BONUS!

Pick up your FREE BONUS sweary word coloring pages!

Check out: **www.FckYeahColoring.com**

For more BONUS pages like this...

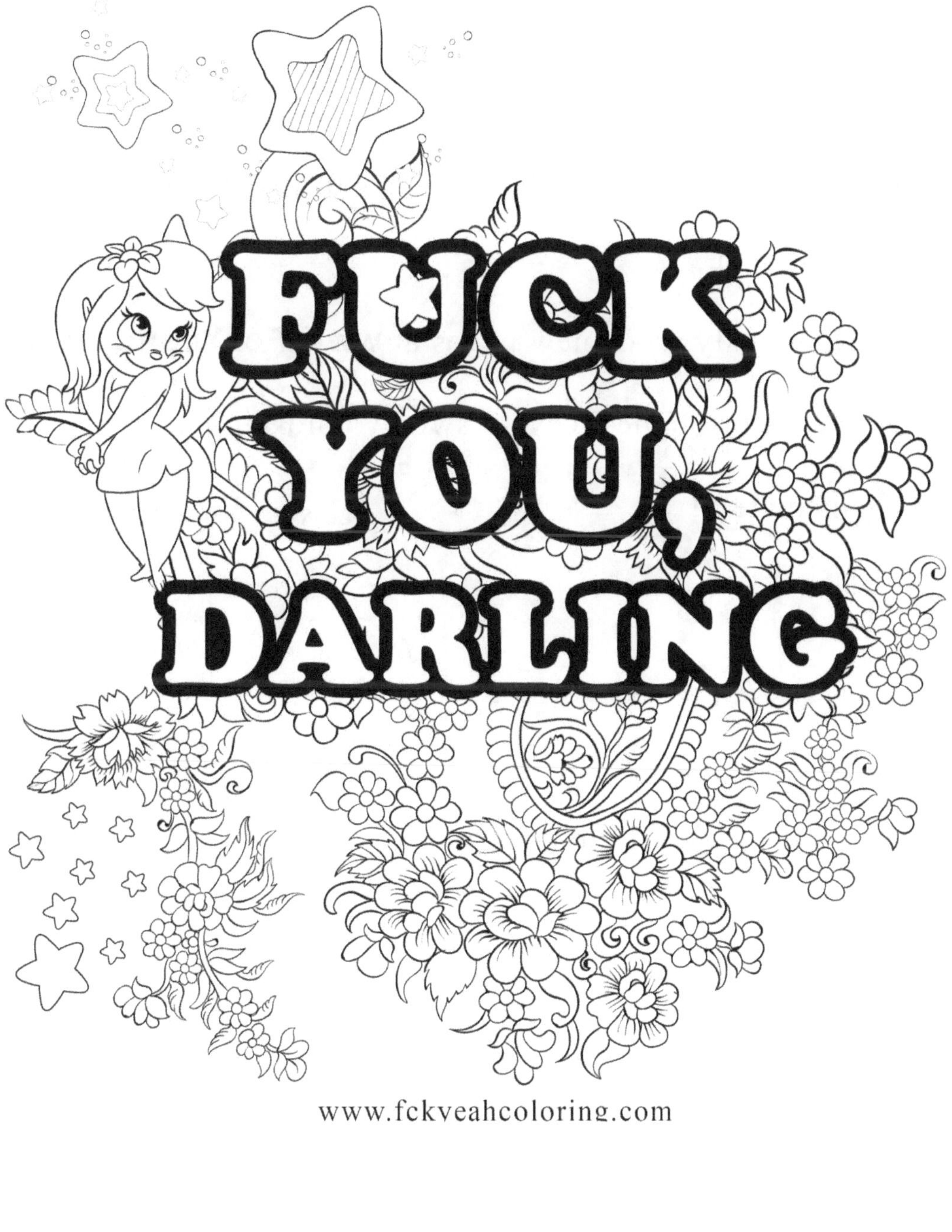

FUCK YOU, DARLING

Dear Creative,

Have a giggle and blow off some steam!

Look through the pages, and pick out the swears that speak to you at the moment.

Just remember, these pages are 18+ and not for the faint-hearted!

I send out NEW, FREE bonus pages every couple of weeks as a special thank you.

Grab your ridiculously crude new pages at **www.FckYeahColoring.com**

Make sure you get printable BONUS sweary coloring pages delivered immediately!

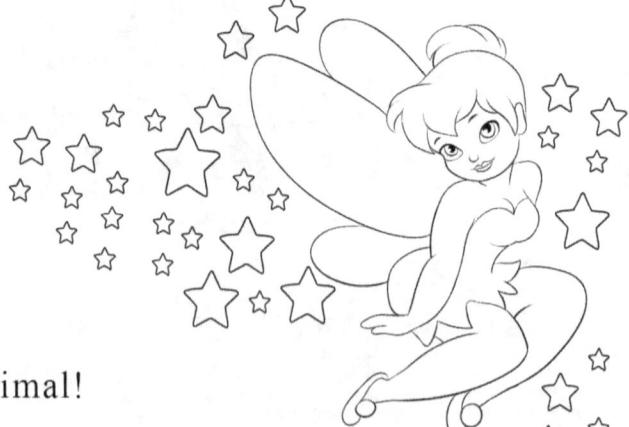

Now, enjoy coloring, you filthy animal!

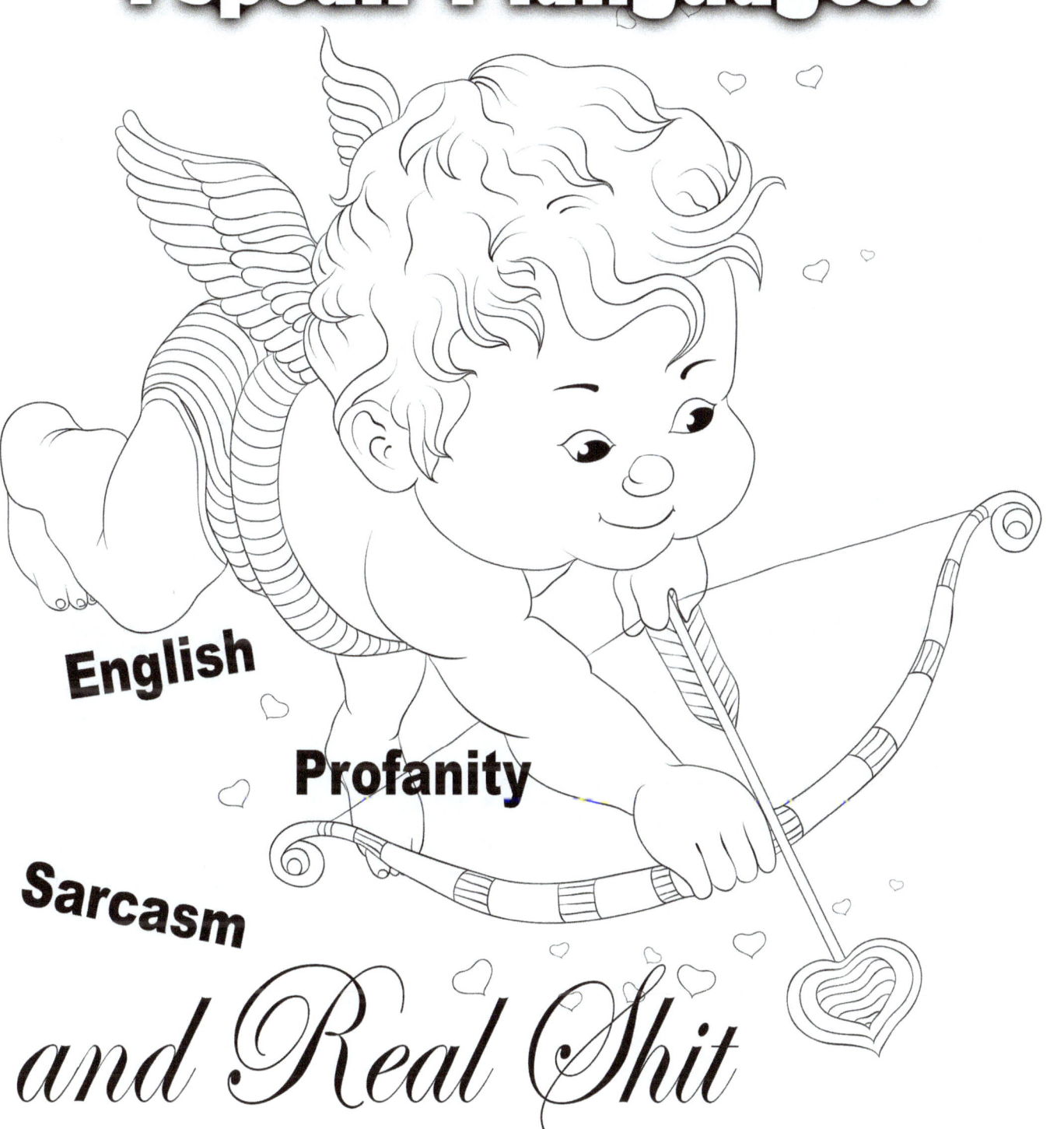

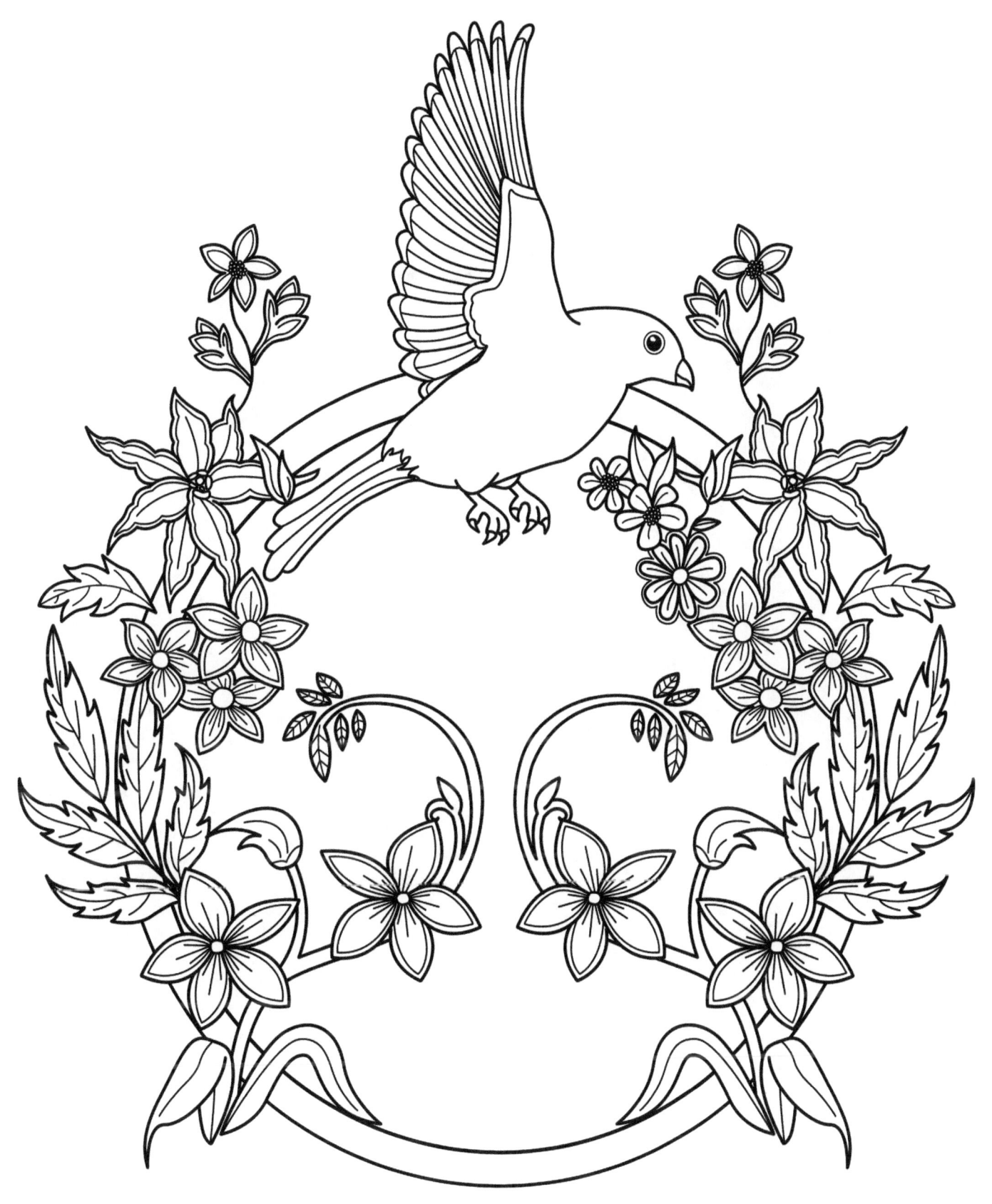

Keep calm and Fuck You

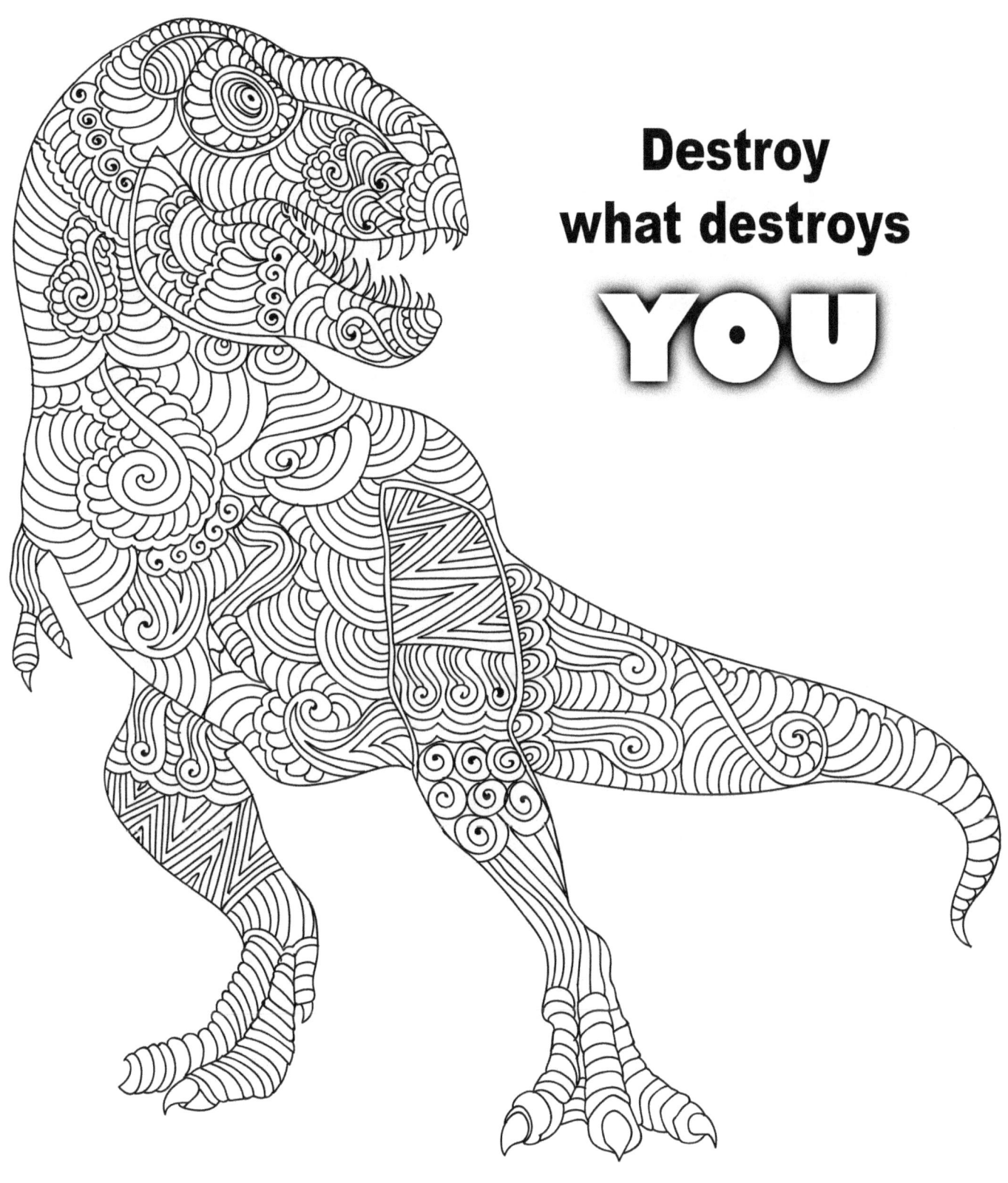

Destroy
what destroys
YOU

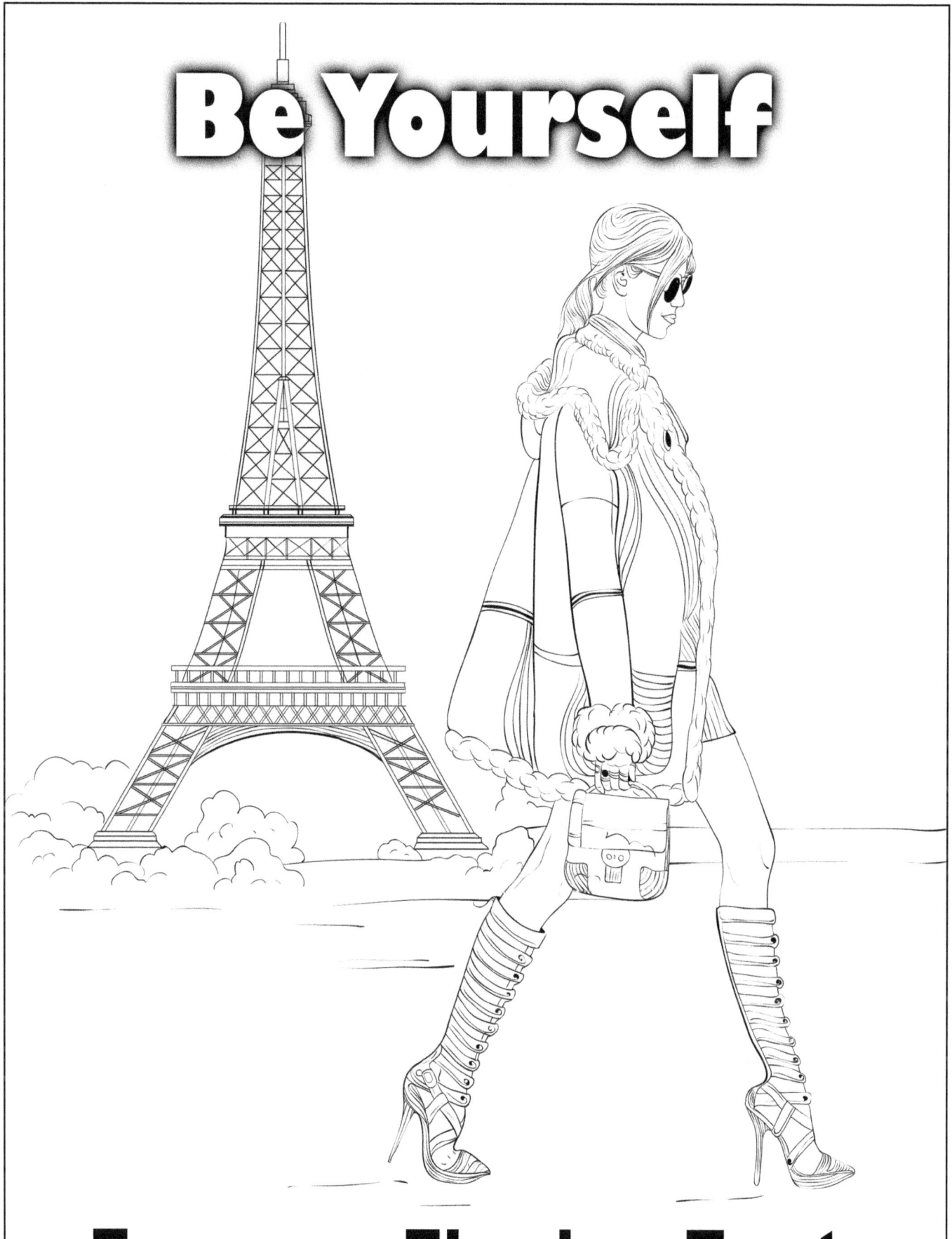

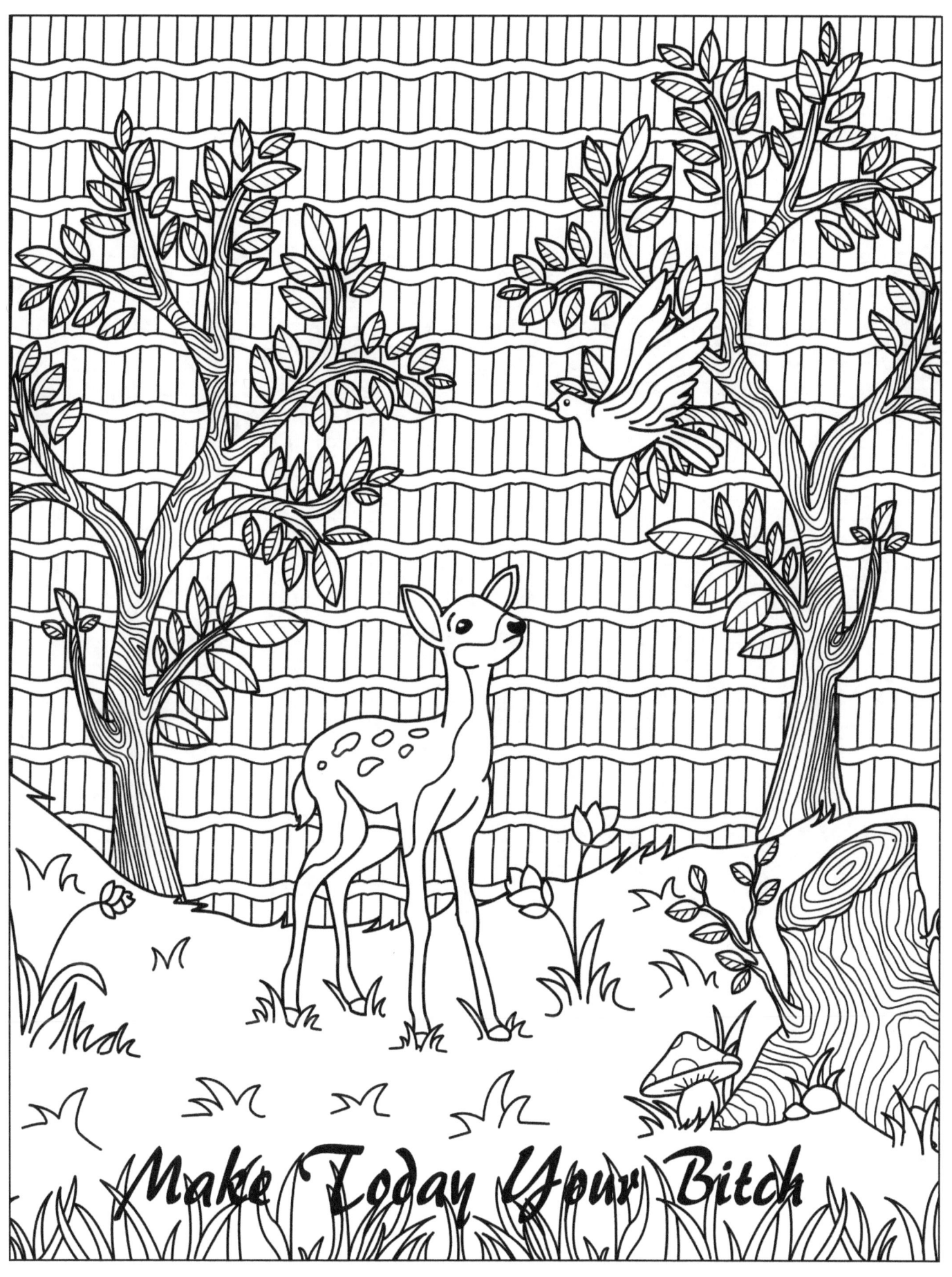

Make Today Your Bitch

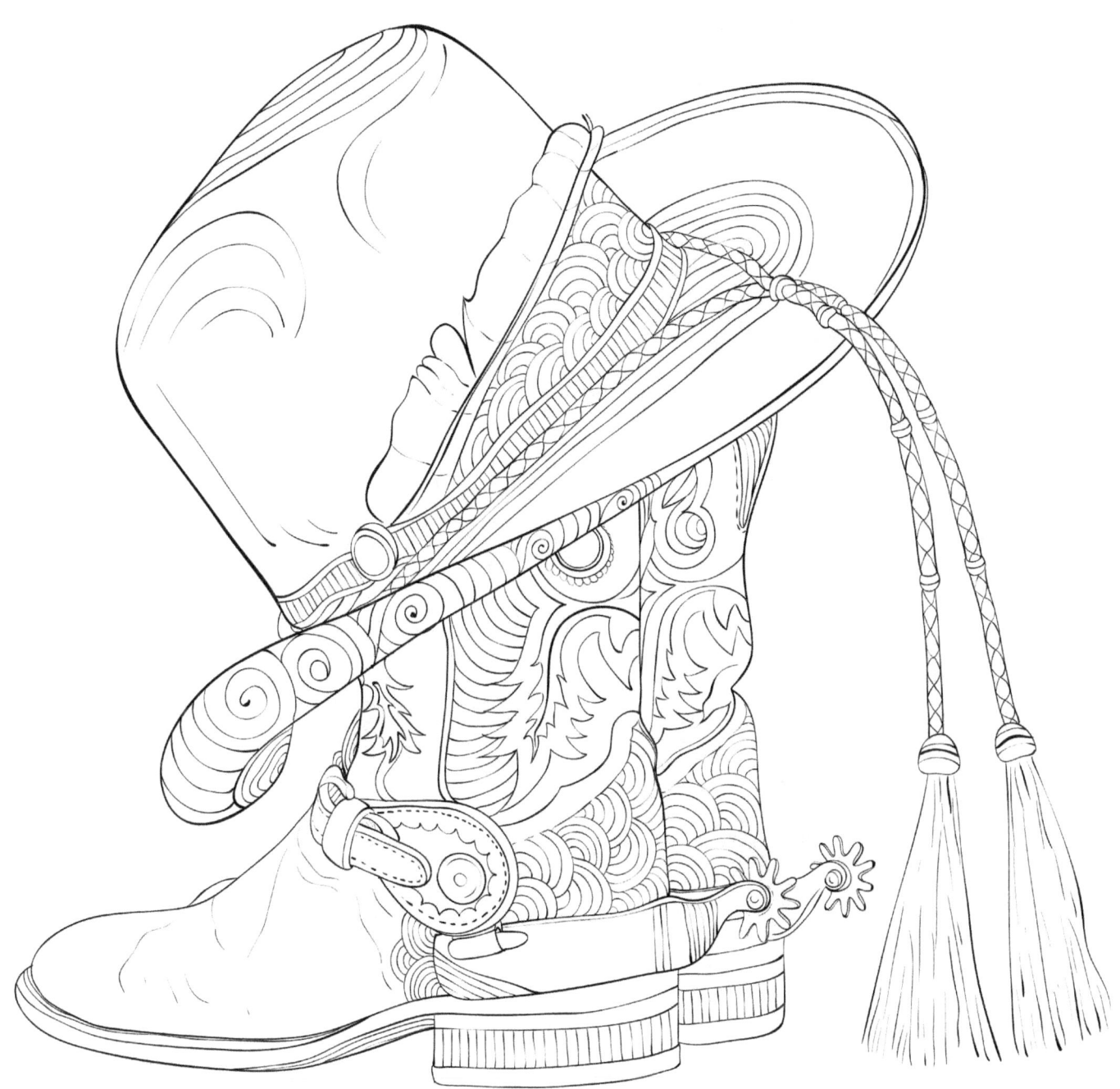

Hakuna Mafuckit

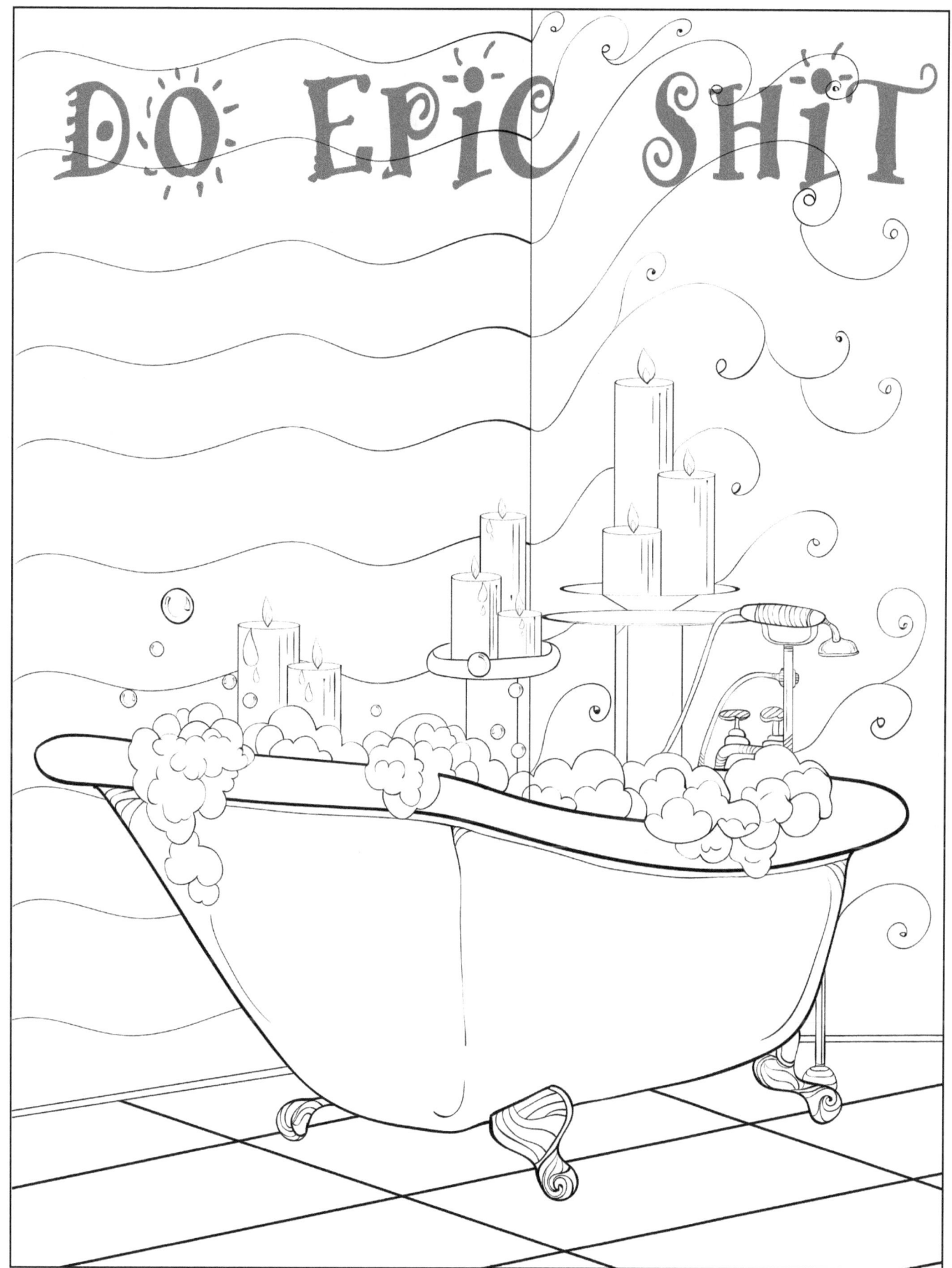

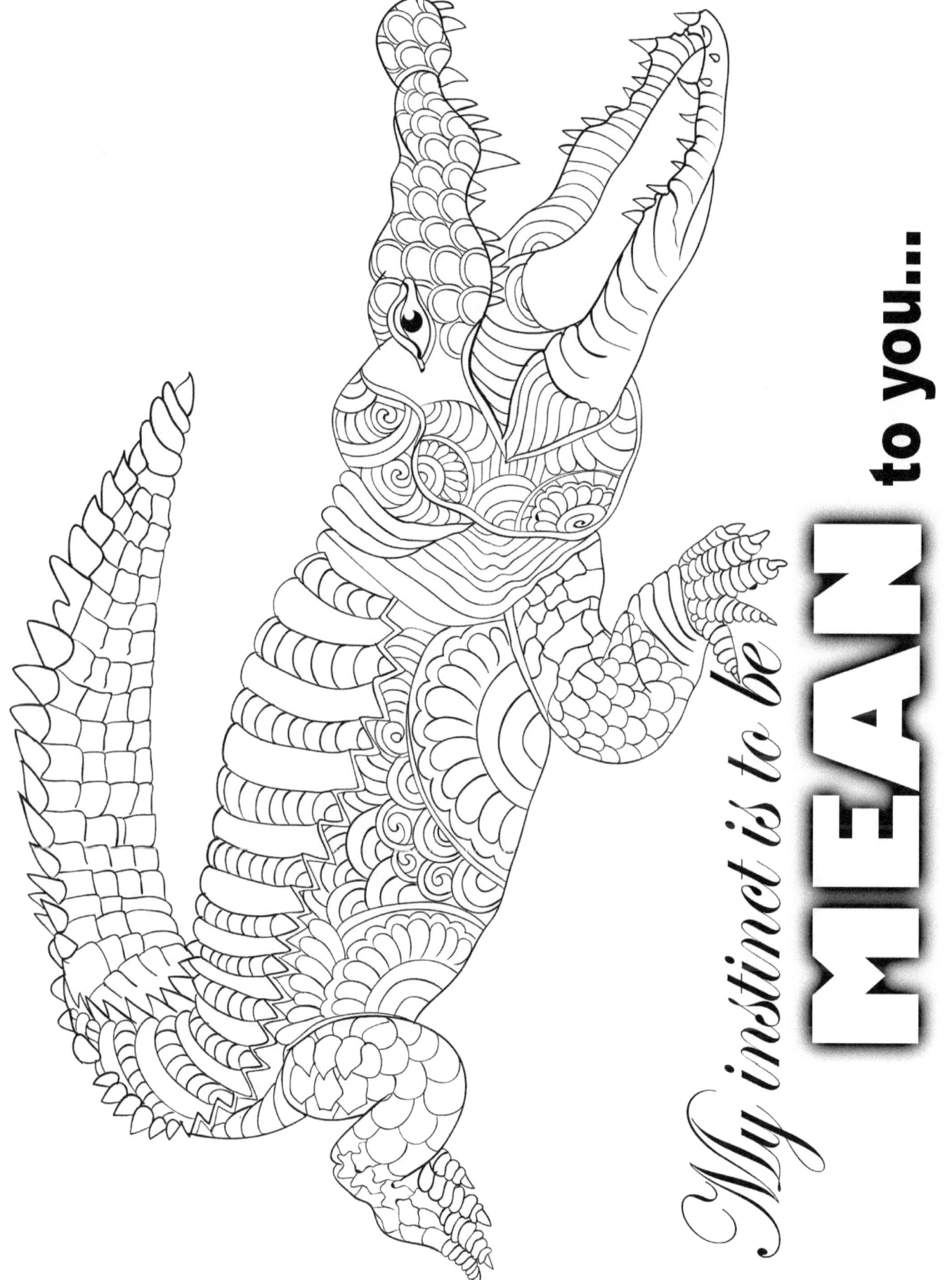

My instinct is to be **MEAN** to you...

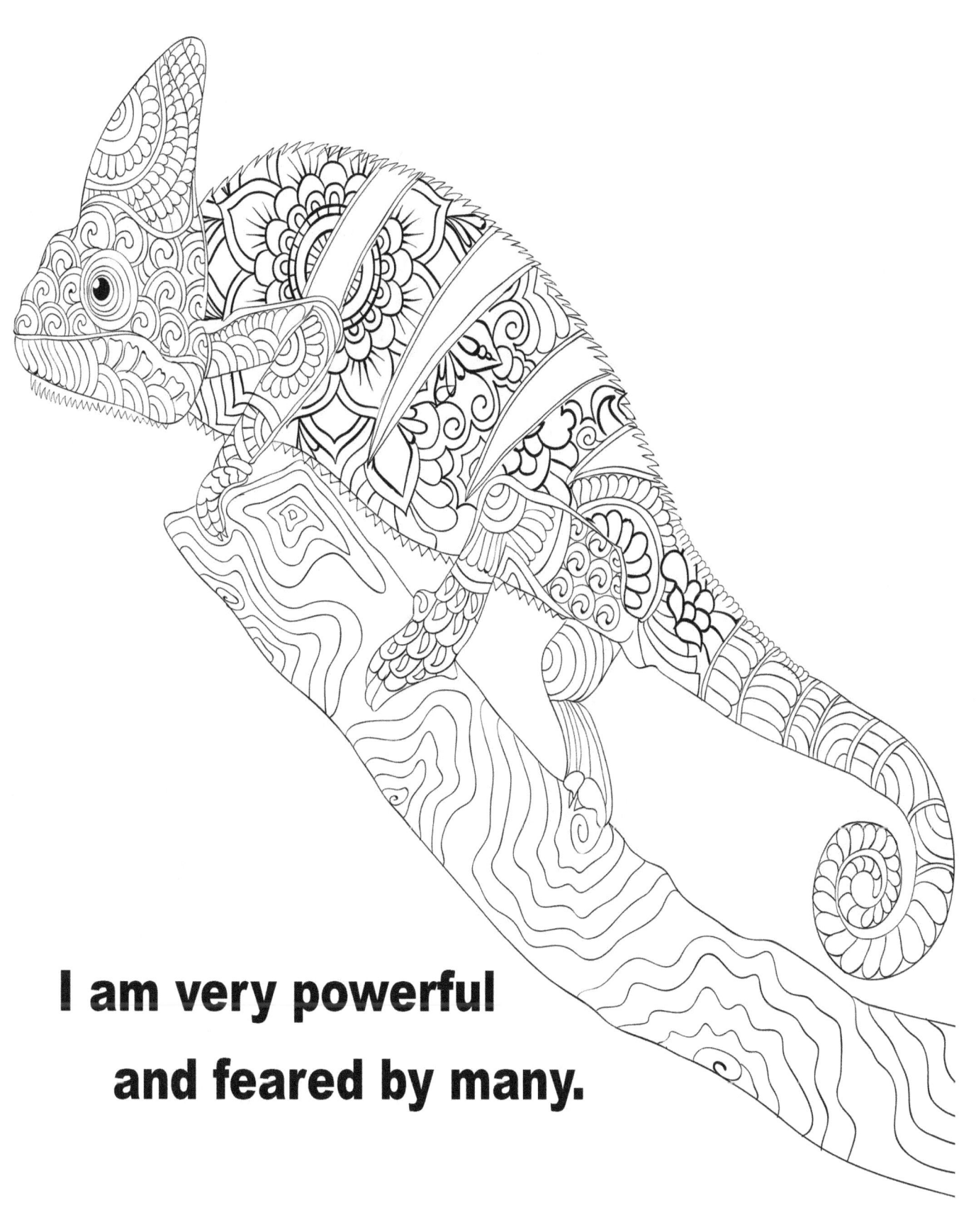

I am very powerful

and feared by many.

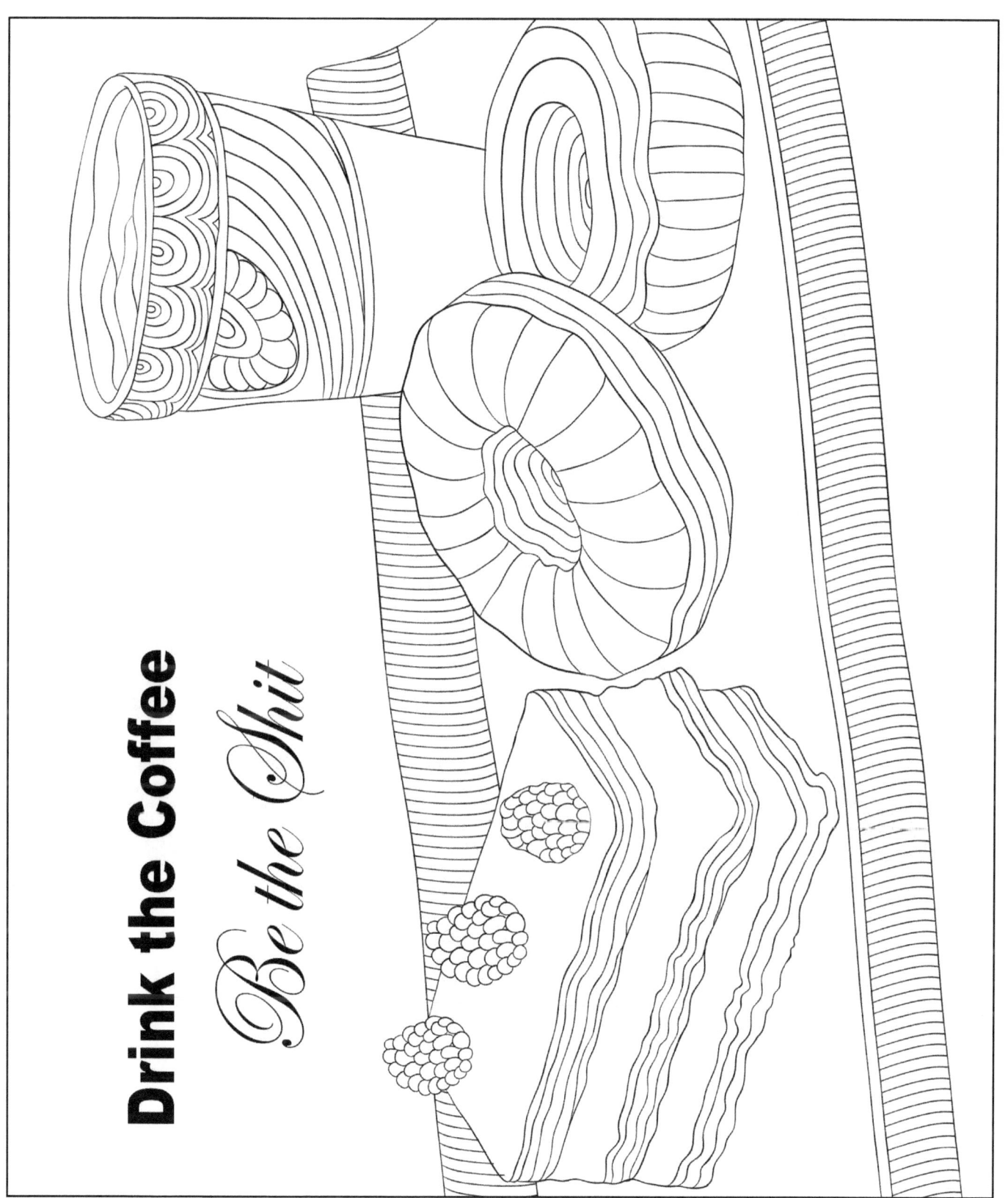

Drink the Coffee

Be the Shit

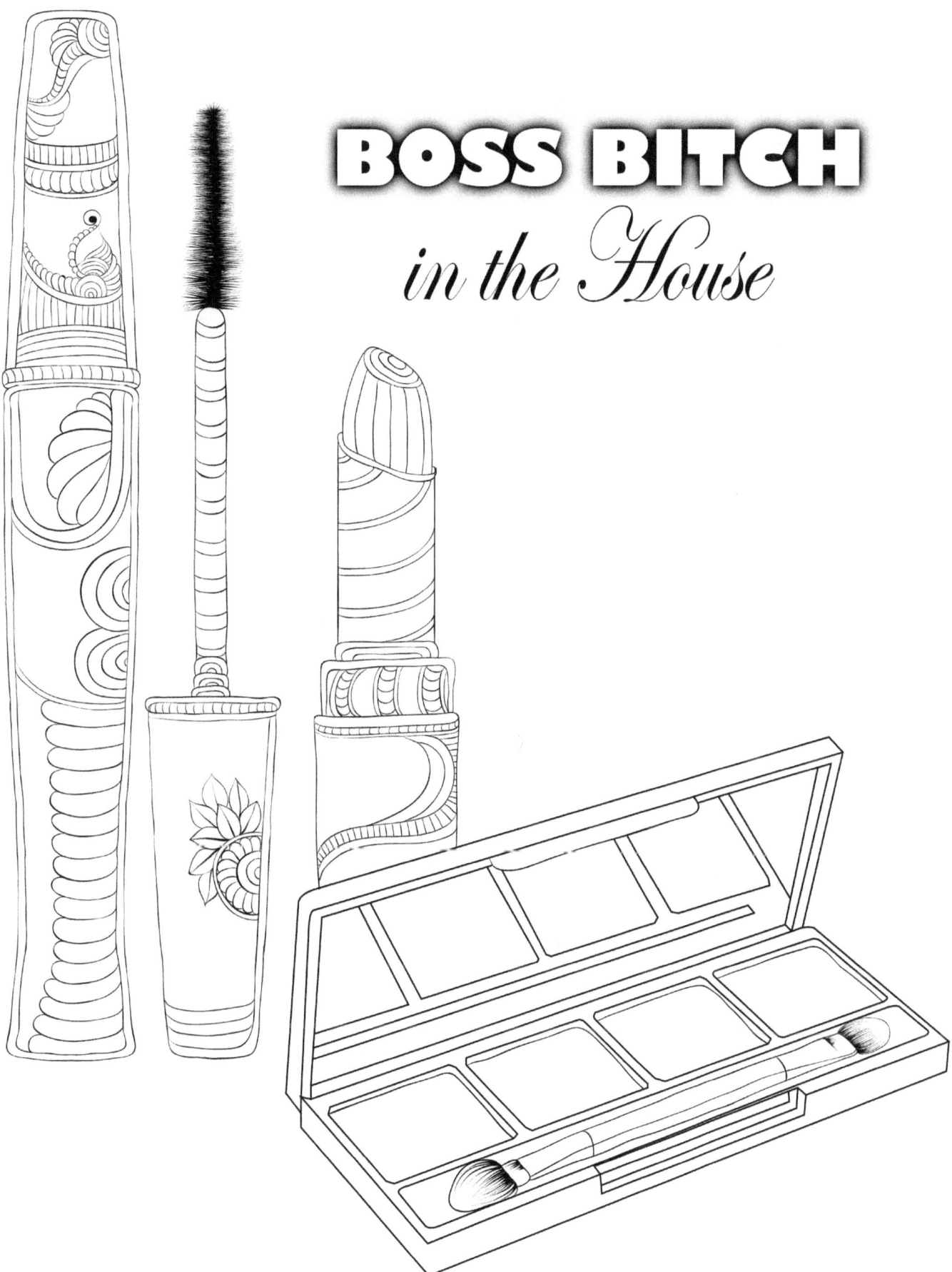

BOSS BITCH

in the House

How 'bout

let's do nothing?

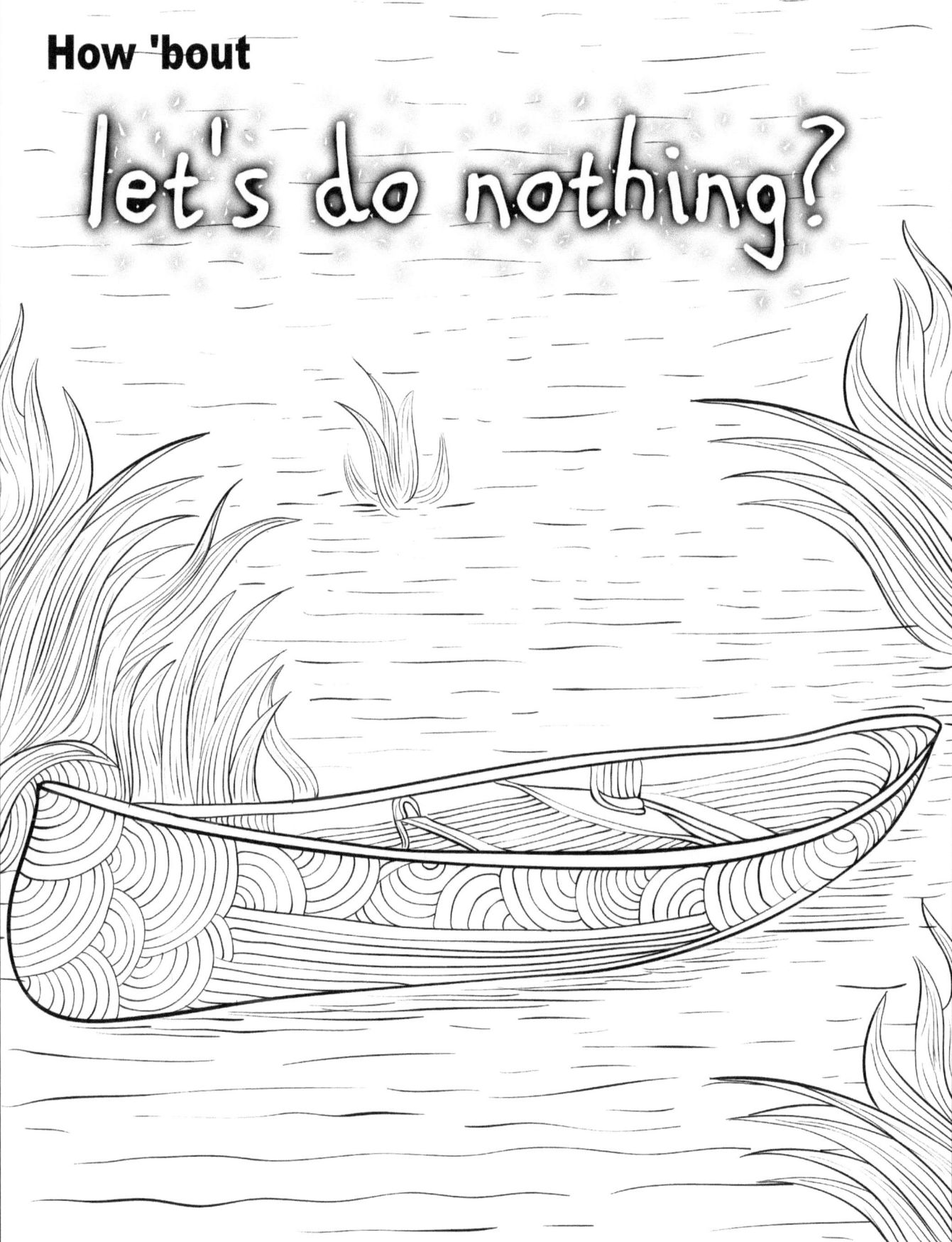

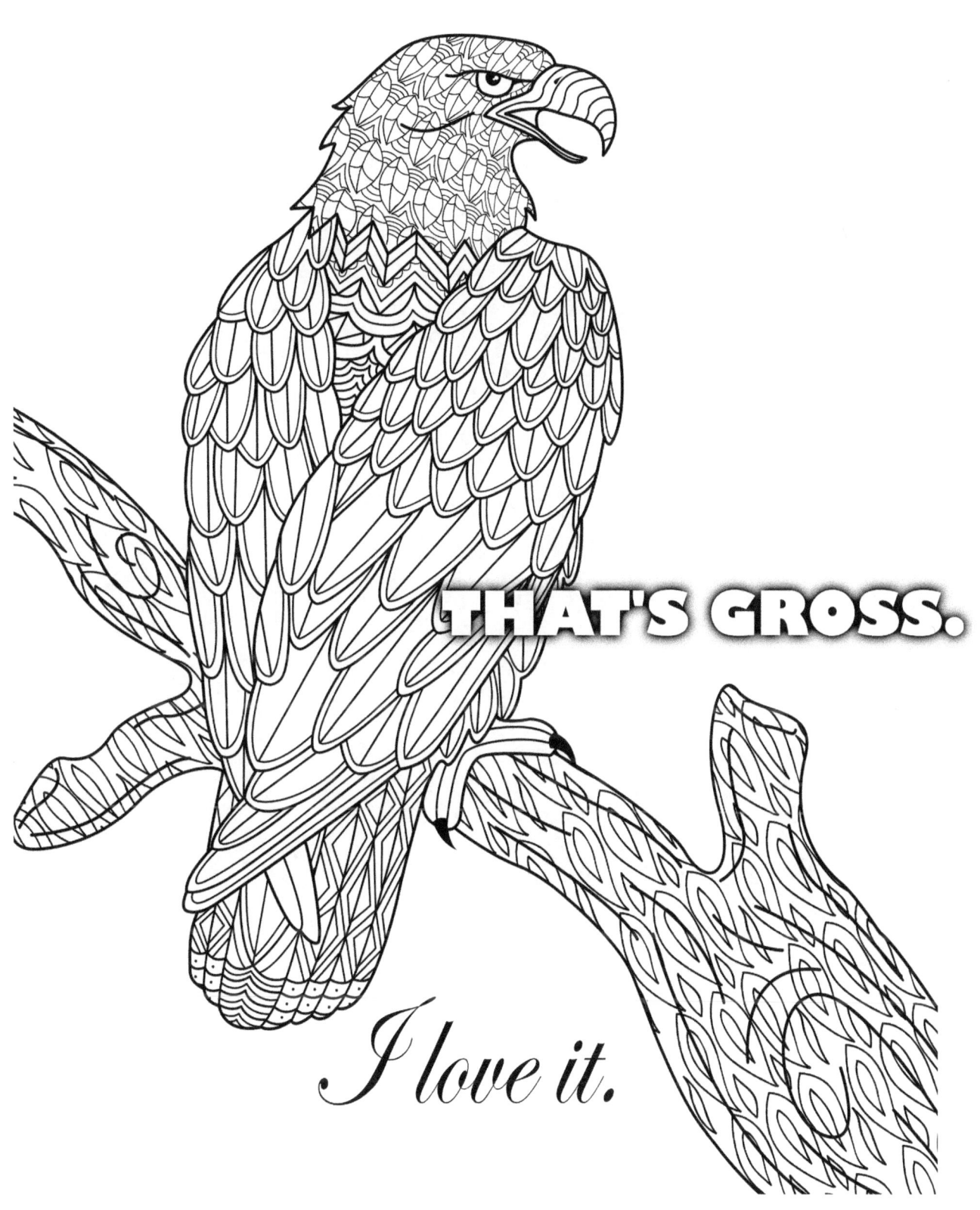

THAT'S GROSS.

I love it.

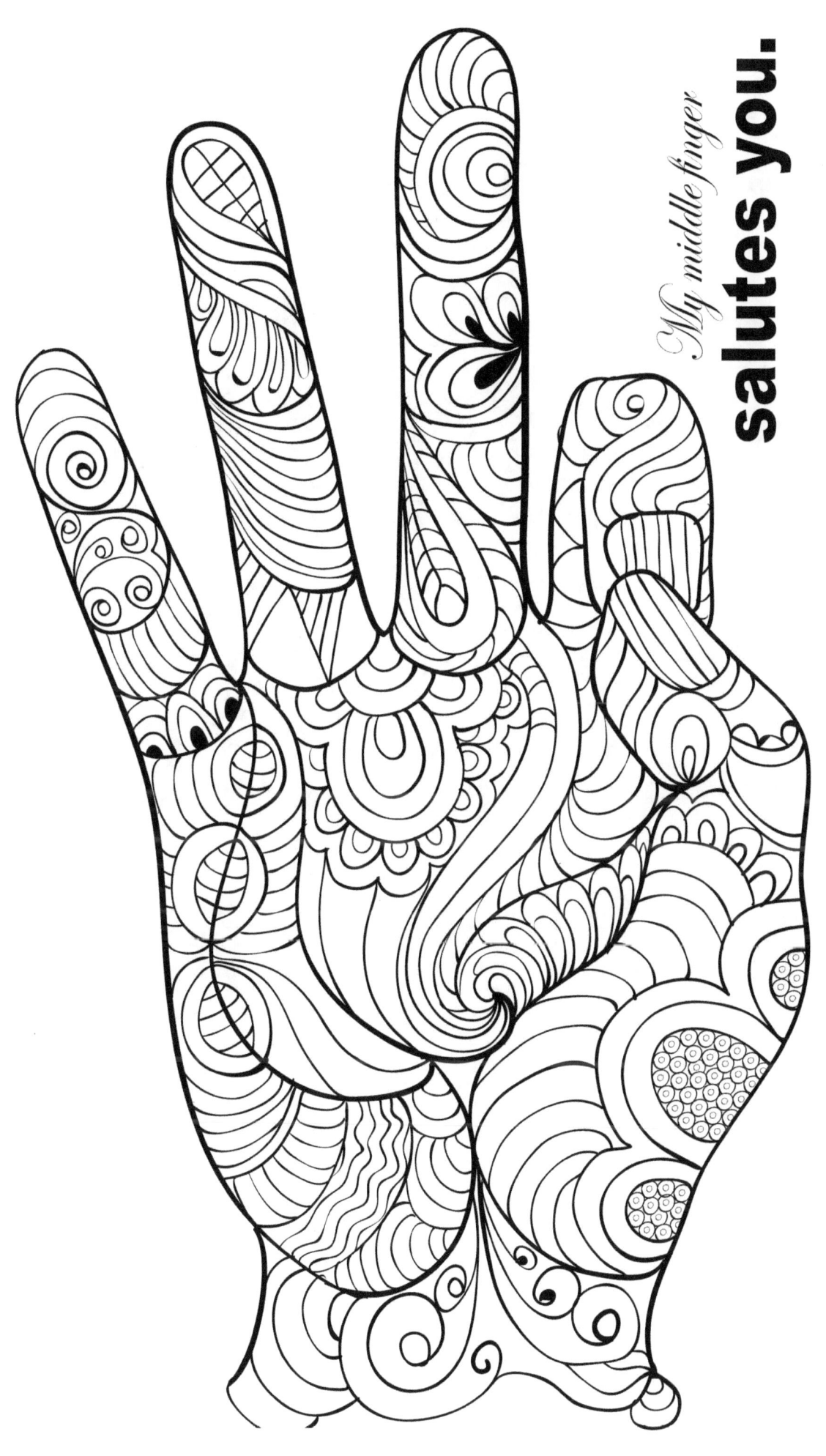

My middle finger **salutes you.**

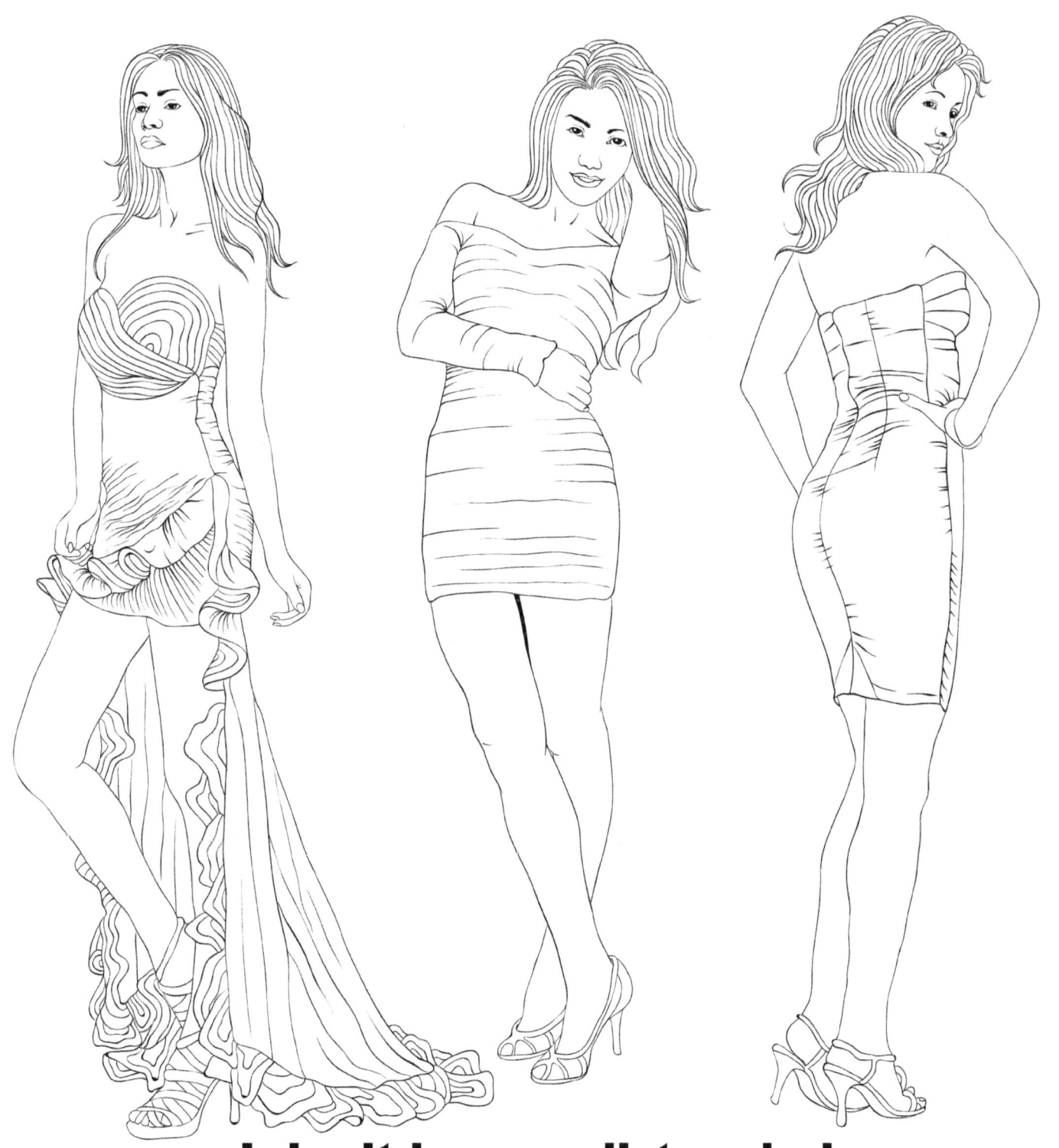

I don't have a dirty mind...
I have a sexy imagination.

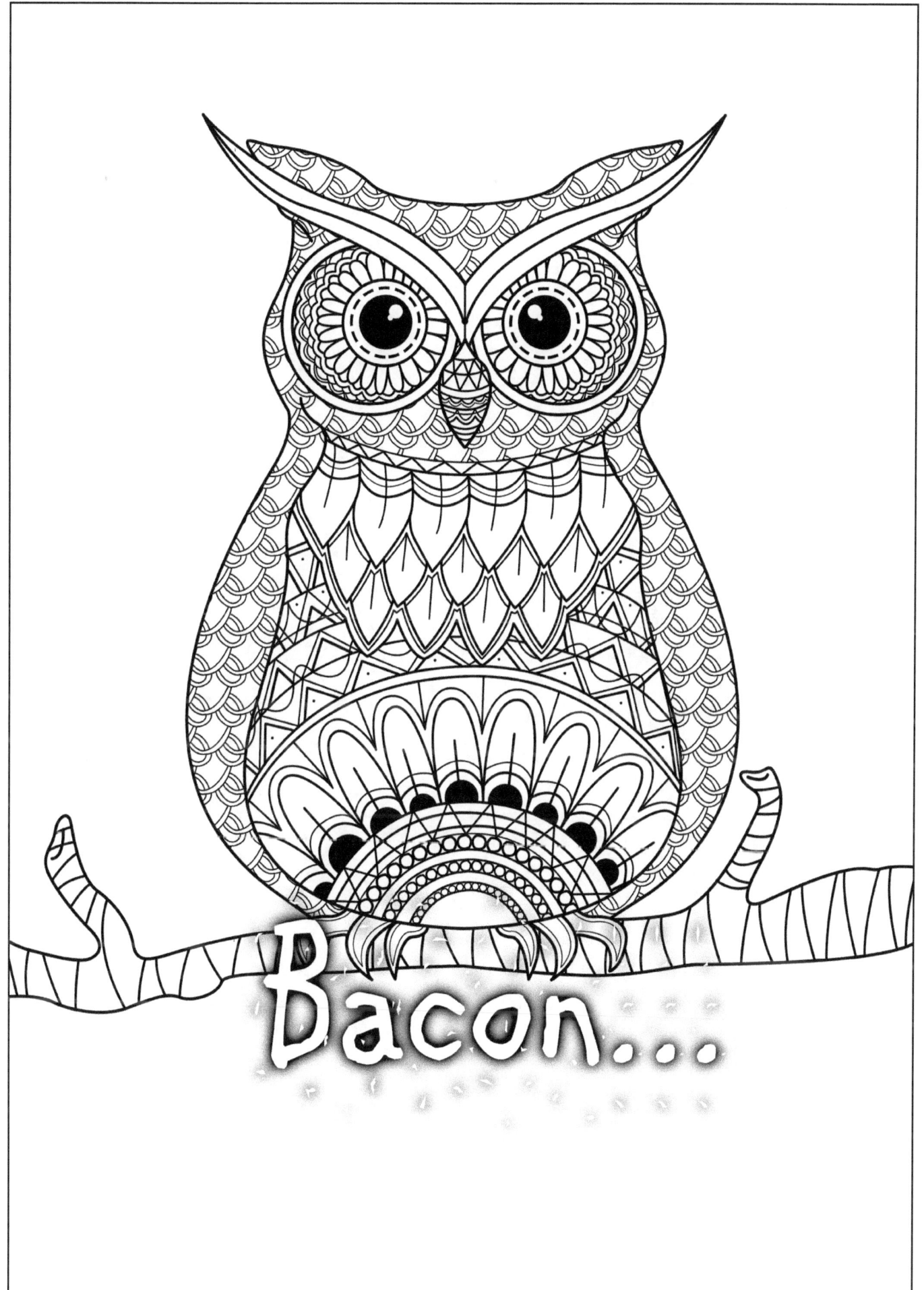

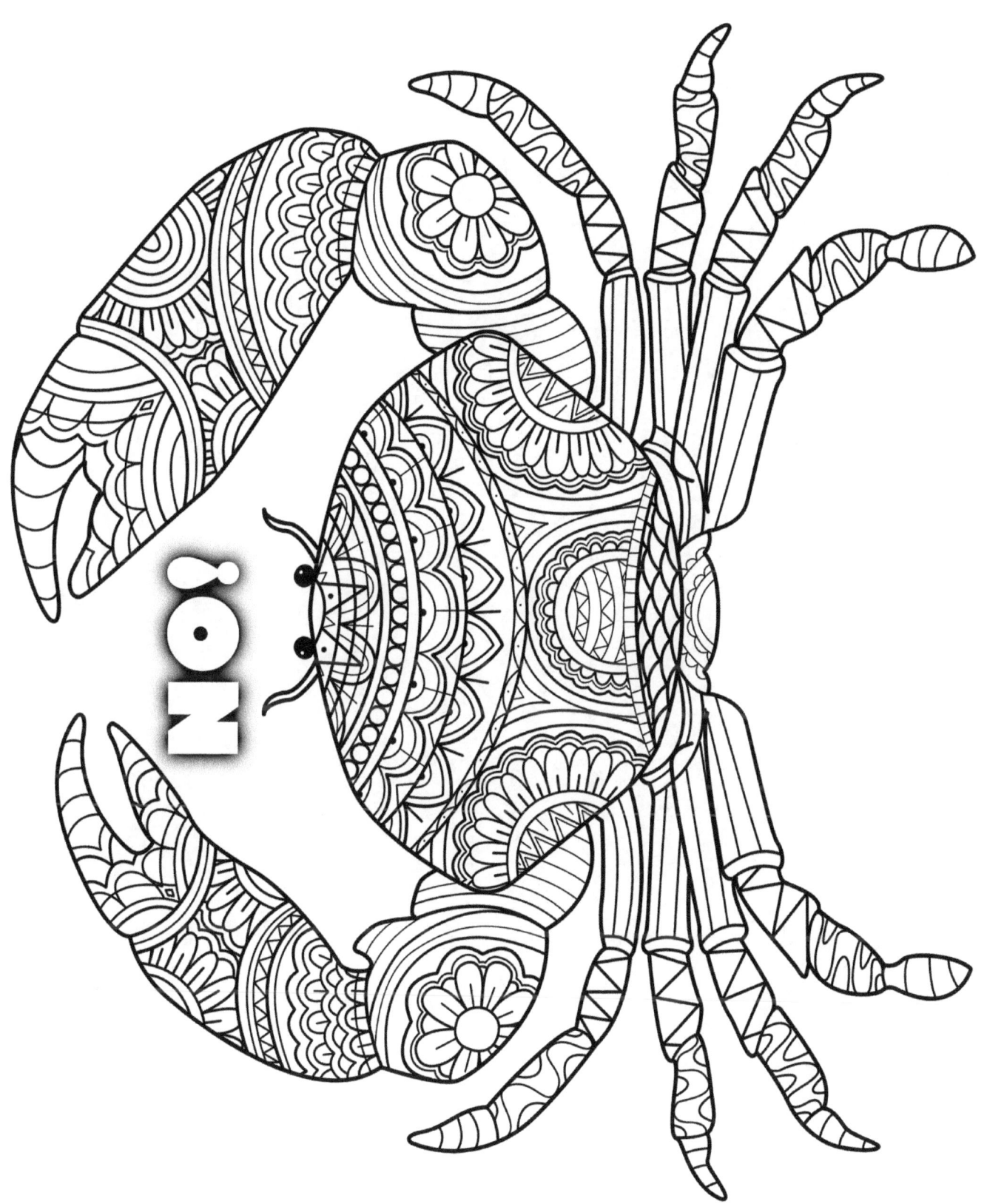

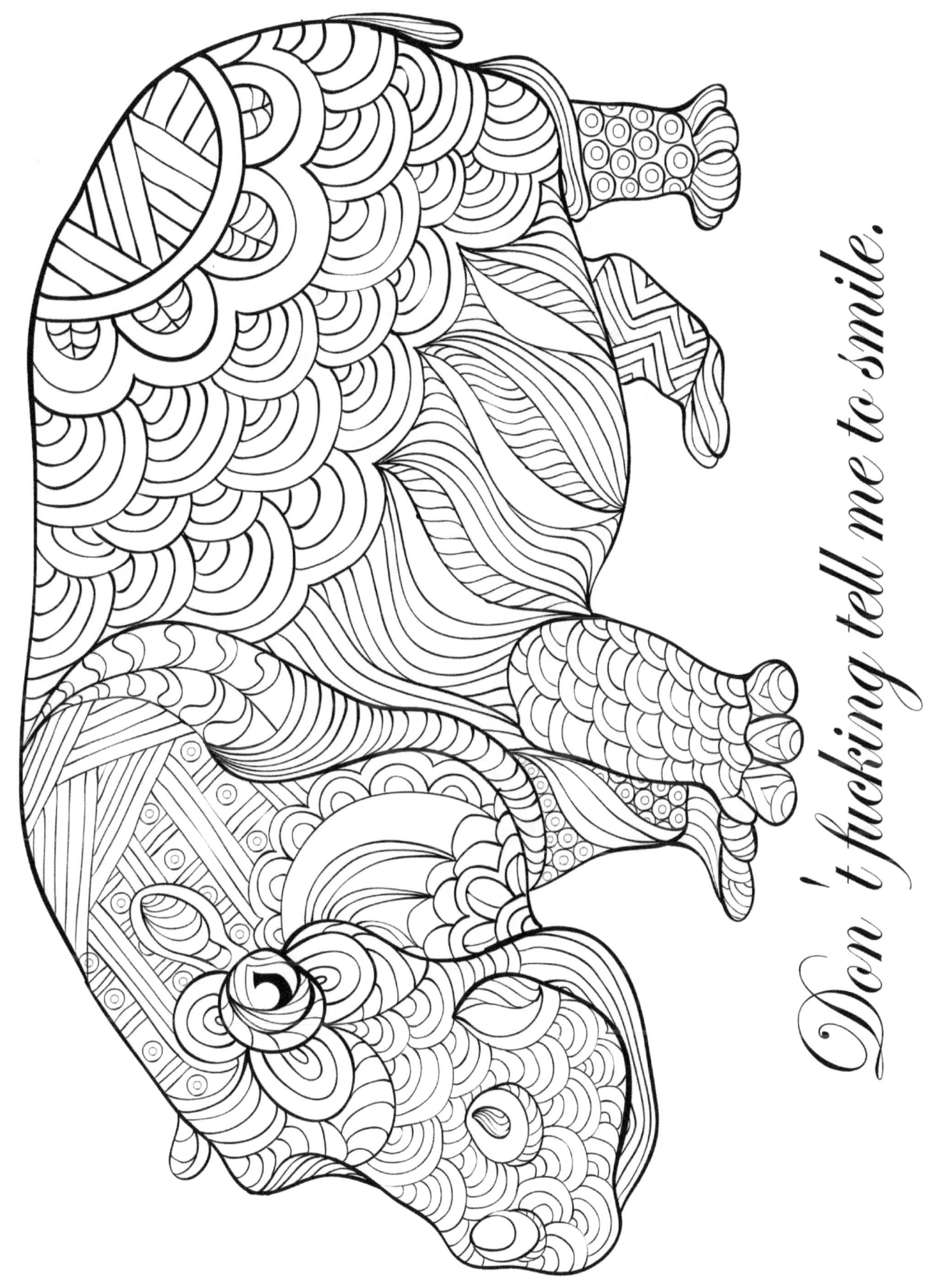

Don' t fucking tell me to smile.

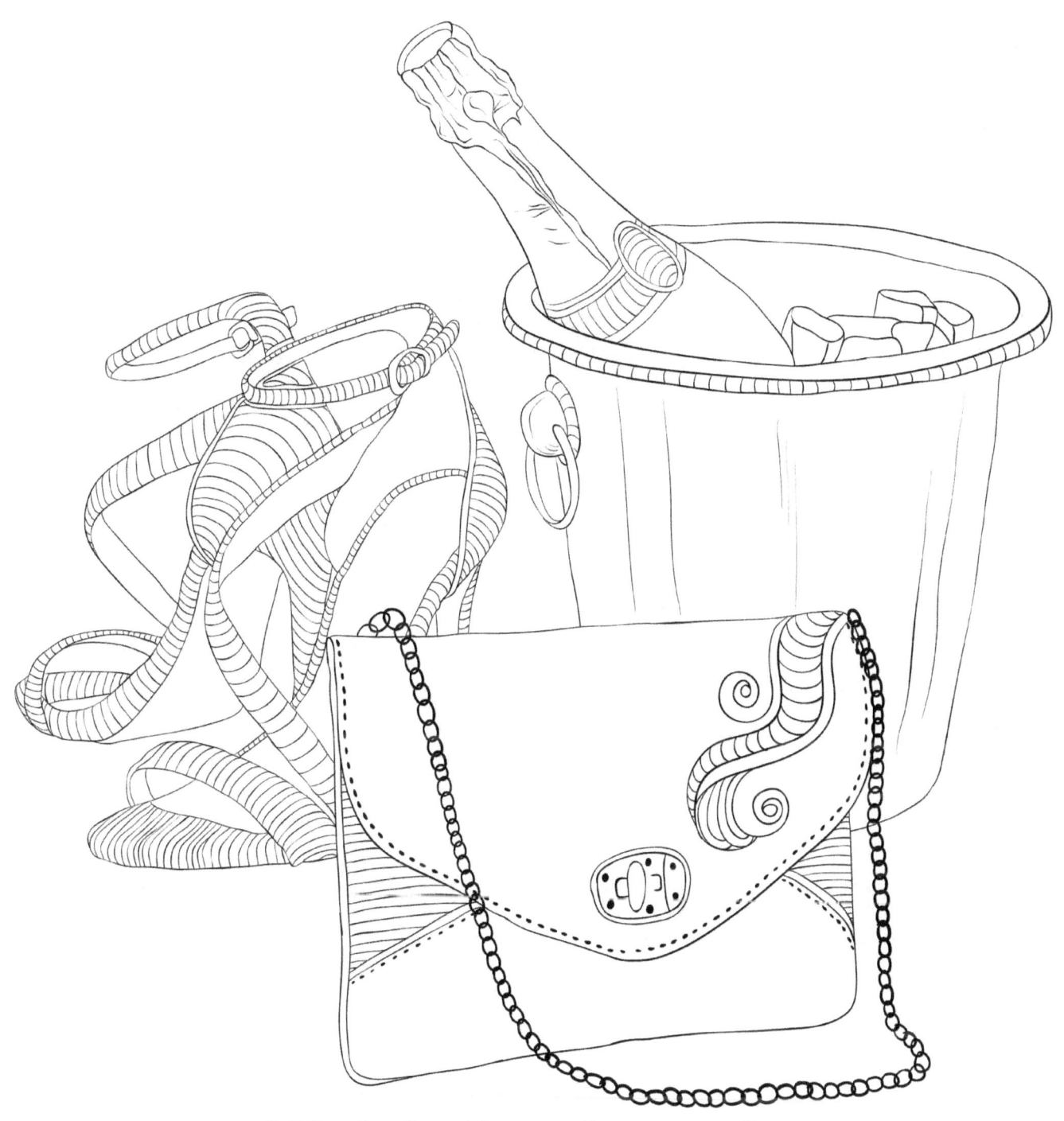

Life is better when you're
DRUNK.

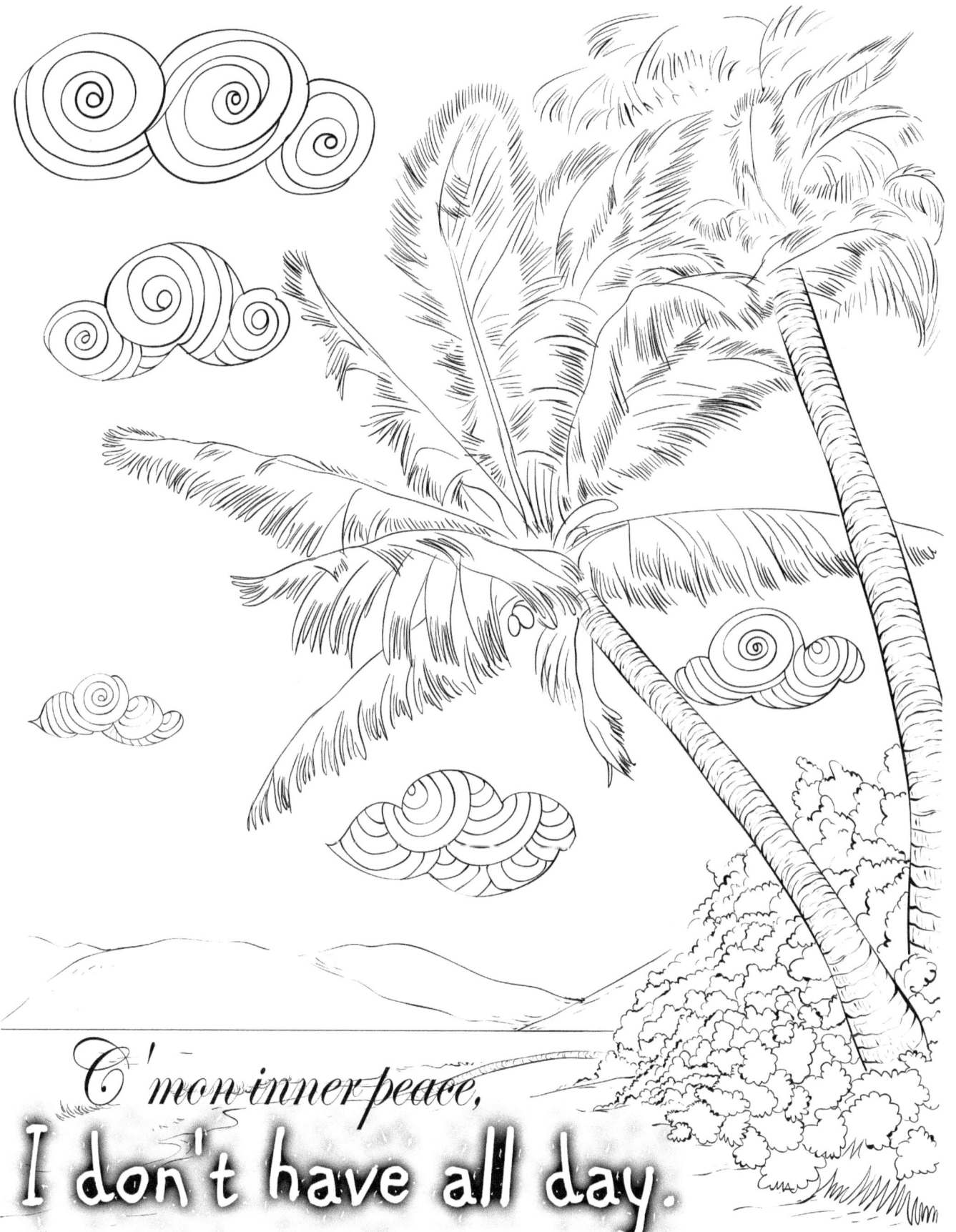

C'mon inner peace,
I don't have all day.

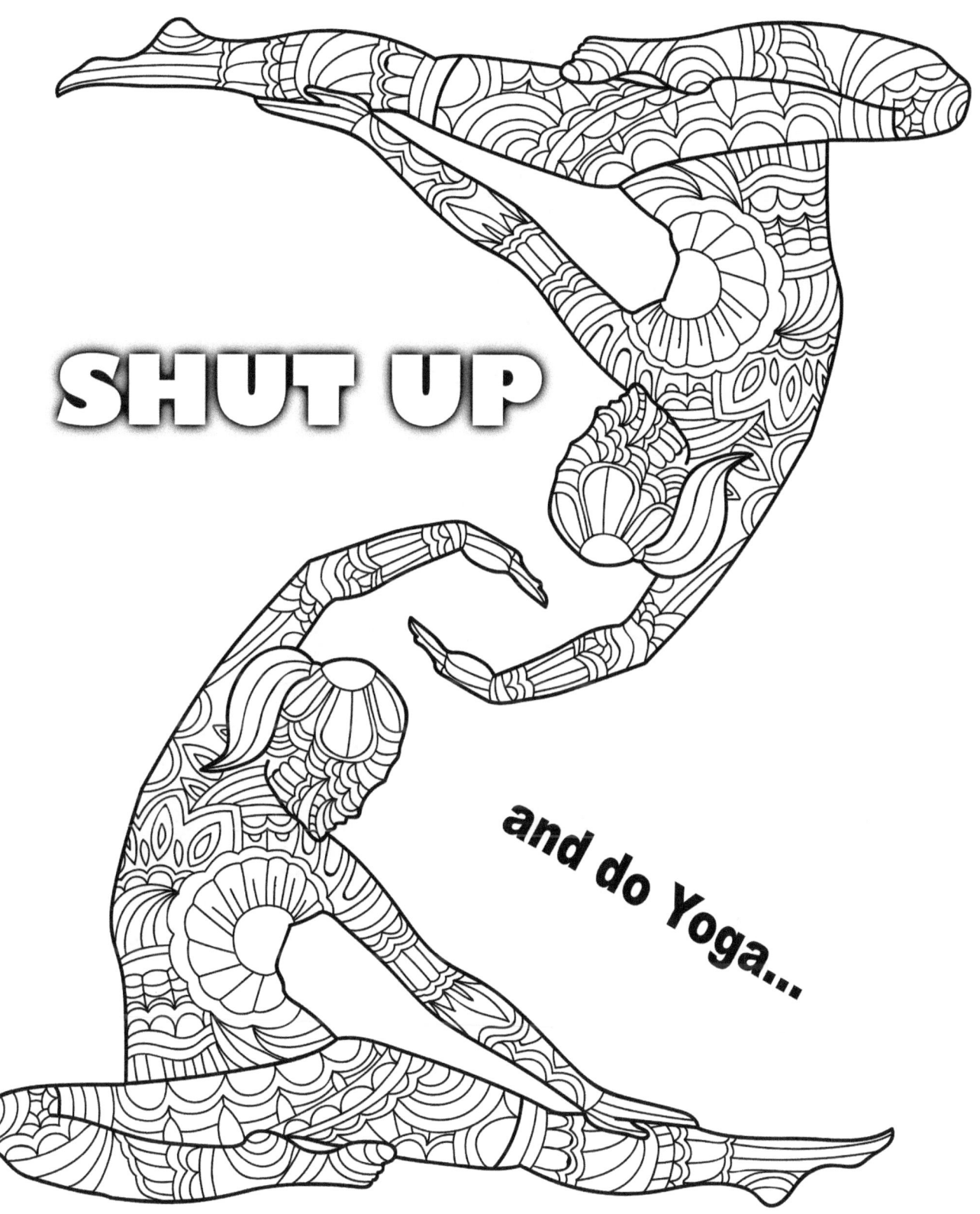

SHUT UP

and do Yoga...

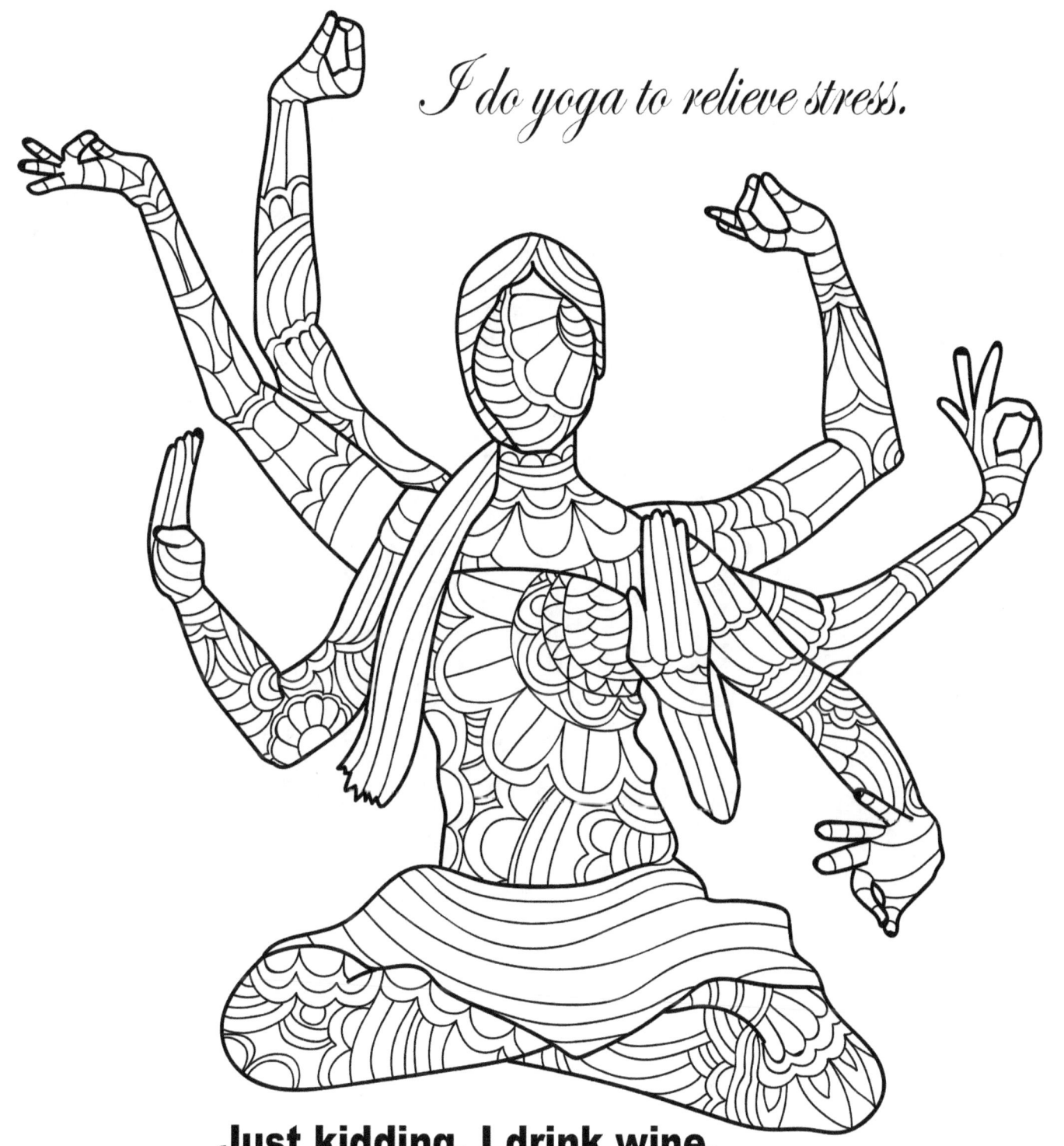

I do yoga to relieve stress.

Just kidding. I drink wine.

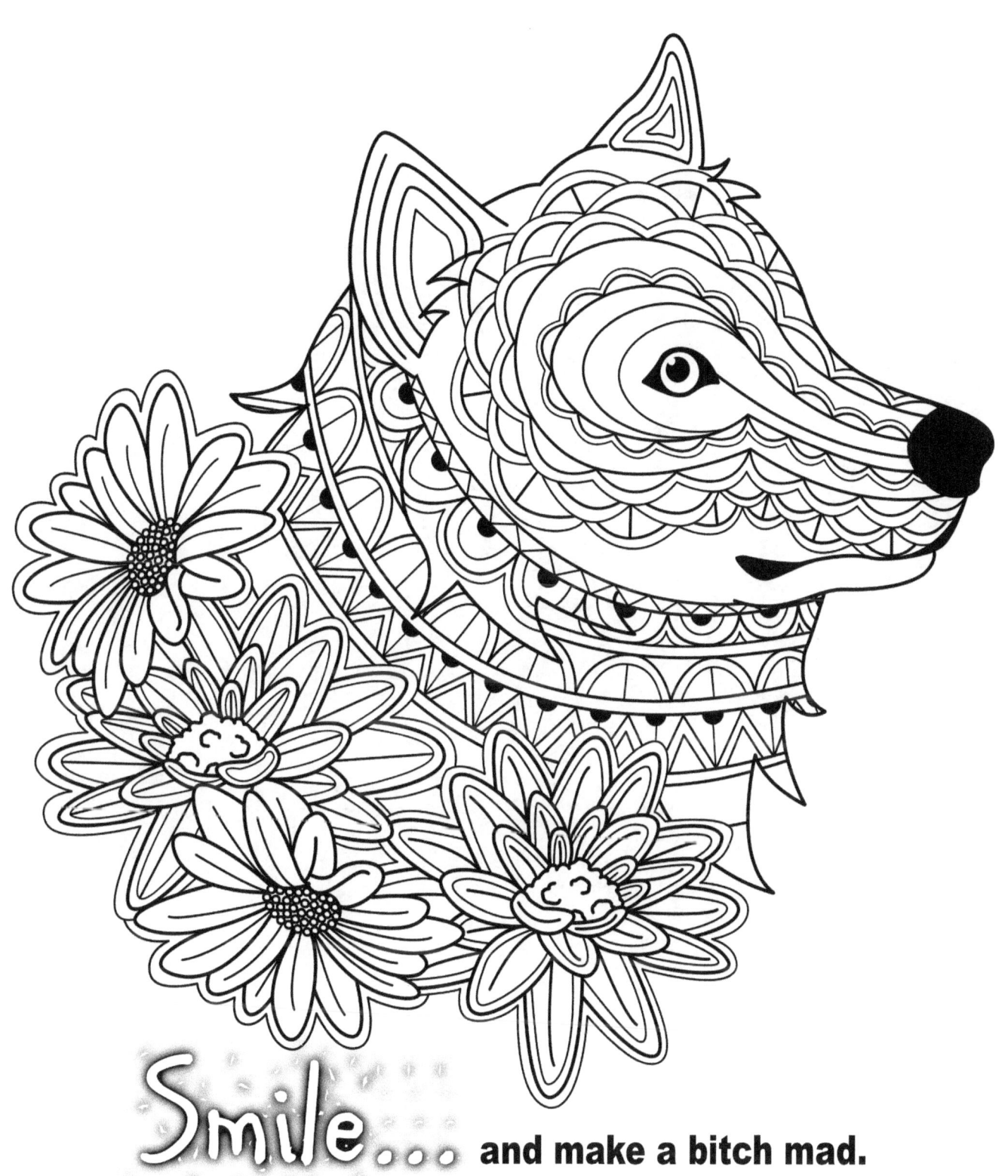

Smile... and make a bitch mad.

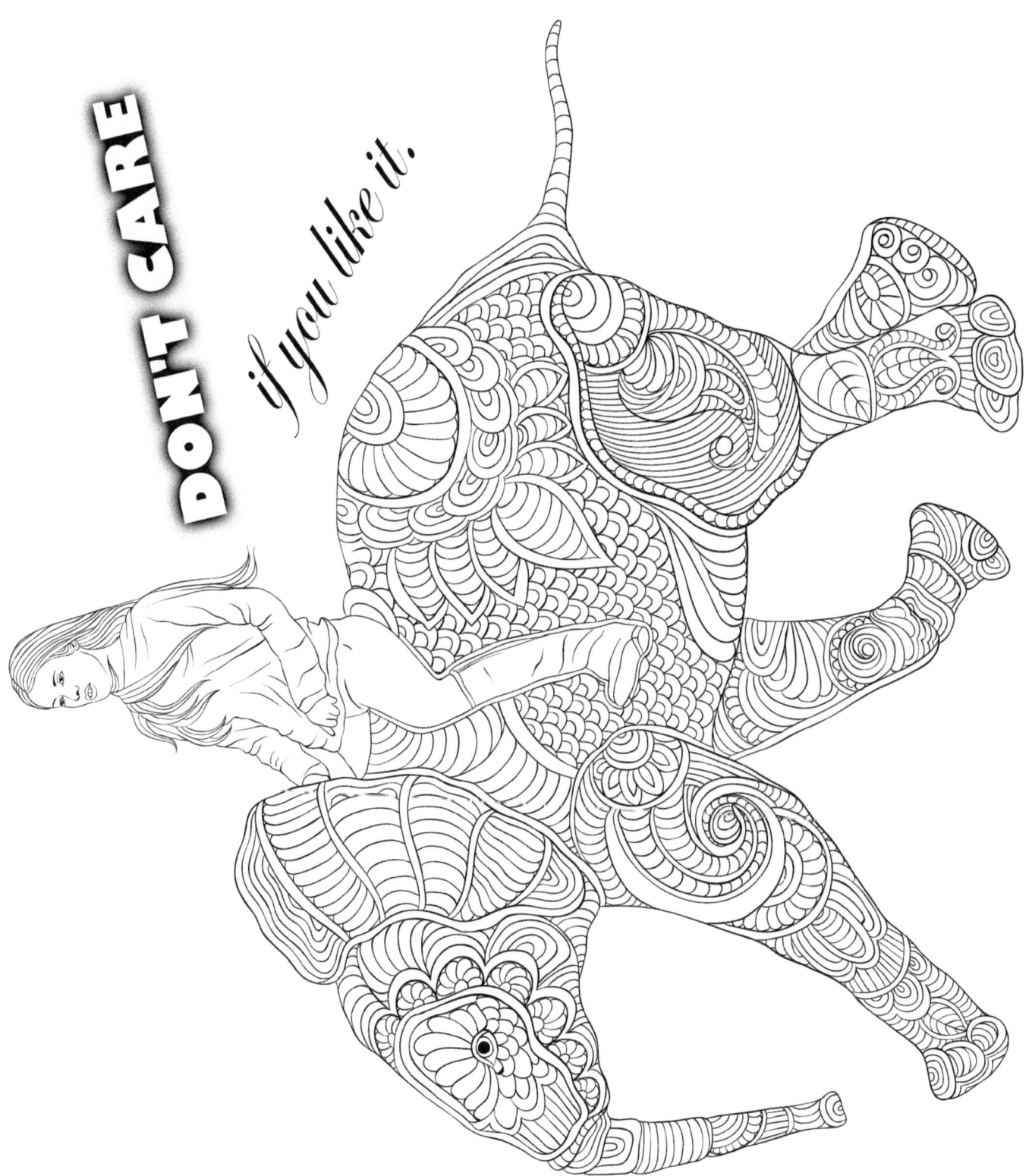

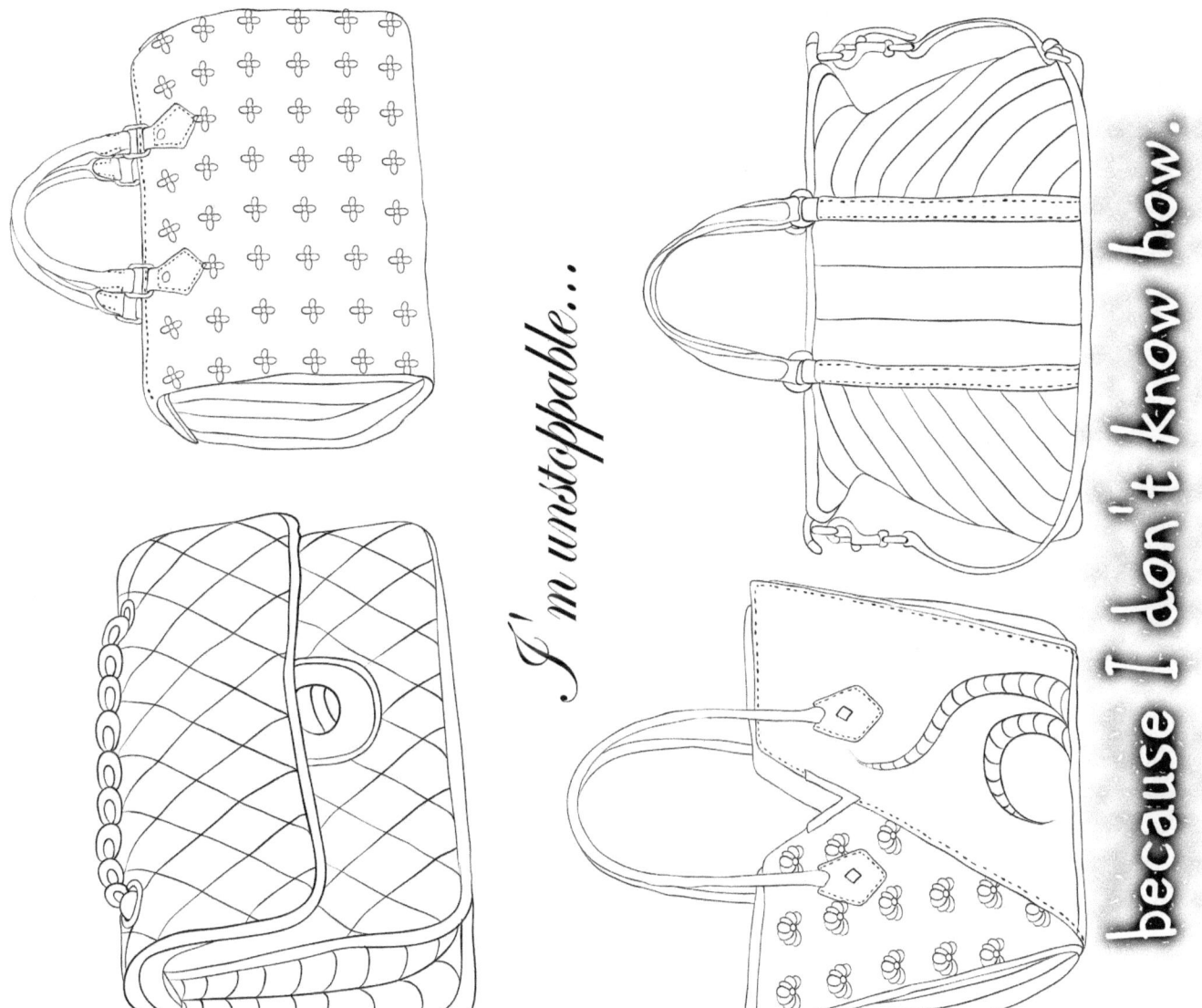

I'm unstoppable...

because I don't know how.

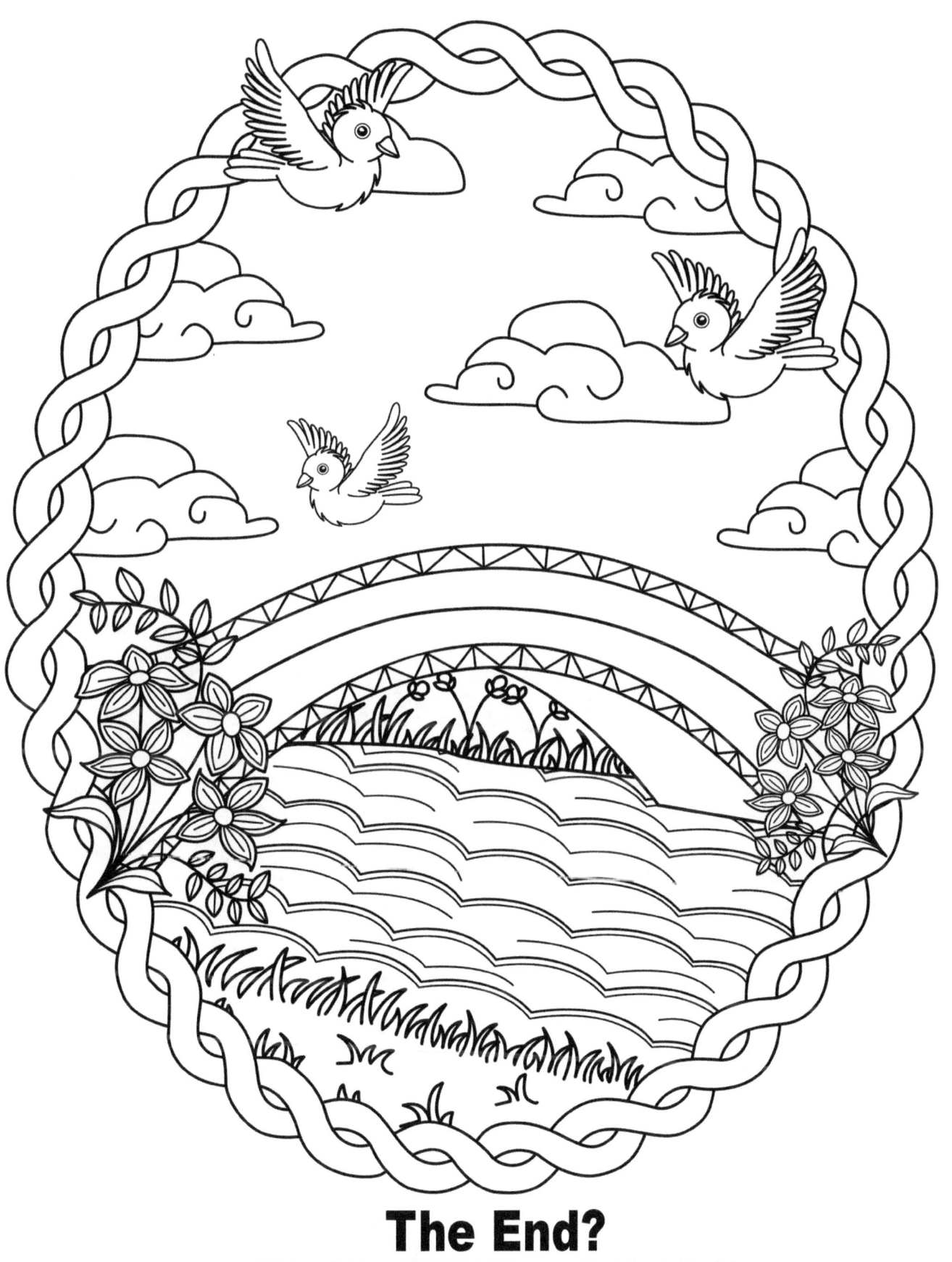

The End?

FUCK, NO!

ISBN: 978-1523734696
Illustrated by:
   Mandala & Caricature Illustration
   Joshua Lazana Lagman and Jade Villaremo

www.ingramcontent.com/pod-product-compliance
Lightning Source LLC
Chambersburg PA
CBHW080634190526
45169CB00009B/3391